Chicks

2, 4, 6

A Baby Animals Counting by Twos Book

by Martha E. H. Rustad

AMICUS READERS ① AMICUS INK

Say Hello to Amicus Readers.

You'll find our helpful dog, Amicus, chasing a ball—to let you know the reading level of a book.

1

Learn to Read

High frequency words and close photo-text matches introduce familiar topics and provide ample support for brand new readers.

2

Read Independently

Some repetition is mixed with varied sentence structures and a select amount of new vocabulary words are introduced with text and photo support.

3

Read to Know More

Interesting facts and engaging art and photos give fluent readers fun books both for reading practice and to learn about new topics.

Amicus Readers and Amicus Ink are imprints of Amicus
P.O. Box 1329, Mankato, MN 56002
www.amicuspublishing.us

Library of Congress Cataloging-in-Publication Data
Names: Rustad, Martha E. H. (Martha Elizabeth Hillman), 1975- author.
Title: Chicks 2, 4, 6 : a baby animals counting by twos book / by Martha E. H. Rustad.
Description: Mankato, MN : Amicus, [2017] | Series: 1, 2, 3 count with me | Audience: K to grade 3._
Identifiers: LCCN 2015041480 (print) | LCCN 2015046553 (ebook) ISBN 9781607539209 (library binding) | ISBN 9781681521114 (pbk.) ISBN 9781681510446 (eBook)
Subjects: LCSH: Counting--Juvenile literature. | Domestic animals--Juvenile literature.
Classification: LCC QA113 .R89 2017 (print) | LCC QA113 (ebook) | DDC 513.2/11--dc23
LC record available at http://lccn.loc.gov/2015041480

Photo Credits: iStock, cover, 8-9, 12-13, 18-19, 24; iStock/aaron007, 1; iStock/Michael Leidel, 3; Shutterstock/Elle1, 5; Dreamstime/Janina Kubik, 6-7; Shutterstock/Halina Yakushevich/10-11; Dreamstime/Sharon Day, 10-11; Alamy/Ed Endicott, 10-11; Shutterstock/Lepas, Elena Butinova, Tony Campbell, Anurak Pongpatimet, Lubava, 14-15; Shutterstock/Erik Lam, 16-17; Shutterstock, 18-19, 24; iStock/Andyworks, 20-21; iStock/bazilfoto, 22-23, 24; Shutterstock/Johannes Kornelius, 22-23

Editor   Rebecca Glaser
Designer   Tracy Myers

Printed in the United States of America

HC 10 9 8 7 6 5 4 3 2 1
PB 10 9 8 7 6 5 4 3 2 1

How many baby animals do you see? Let's count by twos on the farm!

2

Two calves look for their
mother. She will give them
milk.

4

Four foals stand on long legs. Newborn foals can run.

6

Six chicks peck for food. Fluffy feathers keep baby chickens warm.

8

Eight baby goats climb rocks.
They have hard hooves.

10

Ten tadpoles swim.

They will grow into frogs.

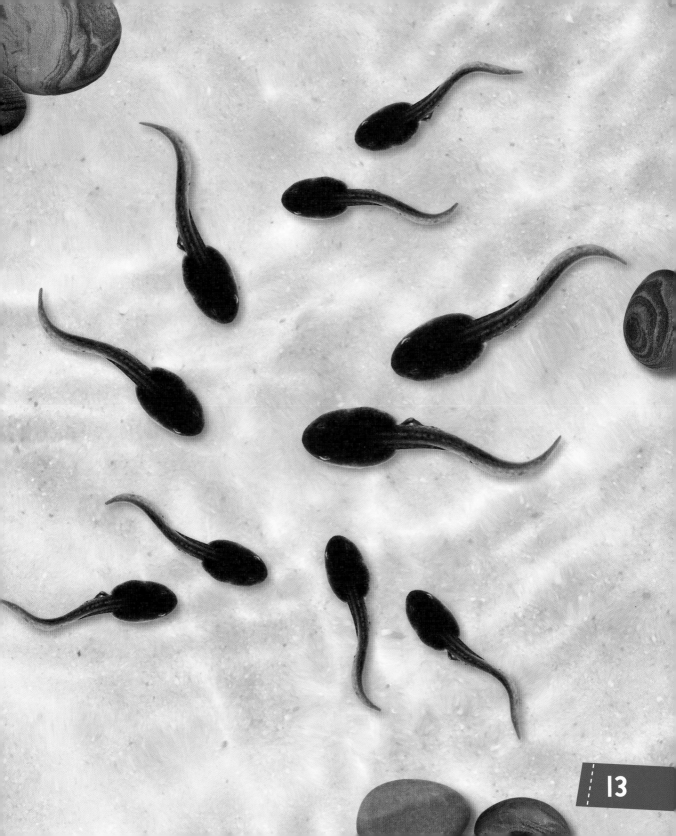

Twelve kittens play. Meow! They pounce to practice catching mice.

12

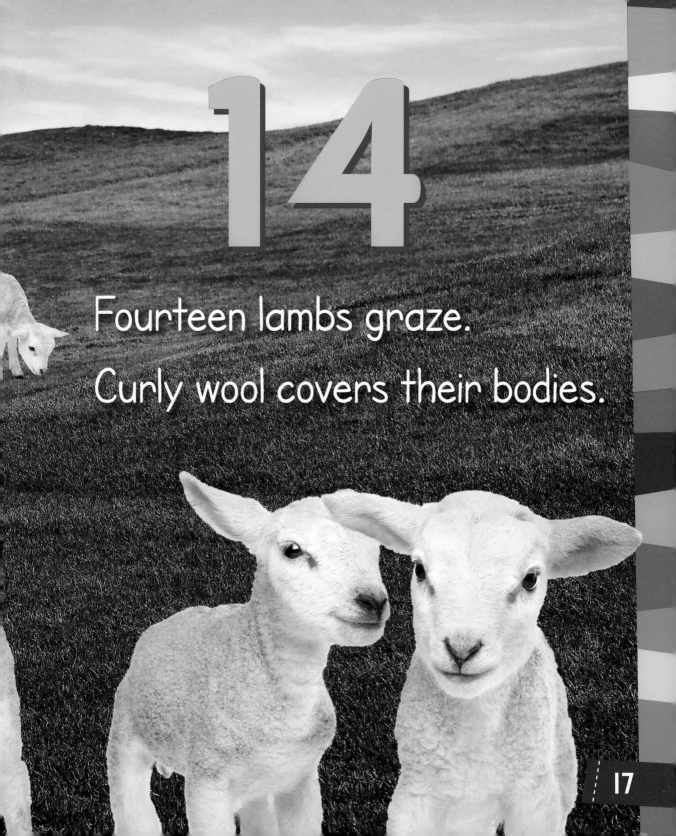

14

Fourteen lambs graze.
Curly wool covers their bodies.

16

Sixteen puppies wait for a bath. Dog shampoo washes dirt away.

18

Eighteen ducklings paddle in a pond. Waterproof feathers keep them dry.

Twenty piglets grunt and squeal. Oink! How many baby animals can you count?

20

Count Again

Count each animal by twos.

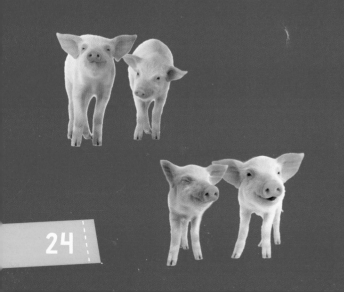